A Guide To Crock Pot Cooking

Theia .S Hardin

All rights reserved. Copyright © 2023 Theia .S Hardin

COPYRIGHT © 2023 Theia .S Hardin

All rights reserved.

No part of this book must be reproduced, stored in a retrieval system, or shared by any means, electronic, mechanical, photocopying, recording, or otherwise, without written permission from the publisher.

Every precaution has been taken in the preparation of this book; still the publisher and author assume no responsibility for errors or omissions. Nor do they assume any liability for damages resulting from the use of the information contained herein.

Legal Notice:

This book is copyright protected and is only meant for your individual use. You are not allowed to amend, distribute, sell, use, quote or paraphrase any of its part without the written consent of the author or publisher.

Introduction

This cookbook offers a convenient and delicious approach to low-carb cooking, with a focus on simple, flavorful dishes prepared in a slow cooker.

The journey begins with Simple Soups and Stews, showcasing comforting classics like Spicy Pumpkin Chicken Soup, Monterey Corn Chowder, and Mexican Crab Bisque. These recipes prioritize ease of preparation without compromising on taste, making them perfect for busy schedules and chilly evenings.

New Chicken Favorites introduces a variety of innovative poultry dishes designed to tantalize taste buds. From Parmesan Crab Stuffed Chicken to Lemongrass Chicken with Zucchini Noodles, each recipe promises a burst of flavor and culinary adventure.

Best Beef Dishes celebrates the richness and versatility of beef, offering mouthwatering options such as Peppery Roast with Beets and Sprouts, Cajun Beef Tips, and Deconstructed Cabbage Rolls. Whether it's a hearty dinner or a special occasion, these recipes deliver on both taste and satisfaction.

Perfect Pork, Veal, and Lamb Dishes explore the savory possibilities of pork, veal, and lamb, with recipes like Herb Garden Stuffed Pork Loin, Garlic Lamb Shanks, and Sweet and Spicy Peachy Pork. These dishes highlight the natural flavors of the meats while incorporating a variety of complementary ingredients for a delightful dining experience.

The section on Variety of Vegetables showcases creative ways to incorporate nutritious vegetables into low-carb meals. From Mexican Mock Mac and Cheese to Slow Cooked Ratatouille, these recipes offer a satisfying blend of flavors and textures that will please even the most discerning palates.

Each recipe in the cookbook is carefully crafted to fit a low-carb lifestyle without sacrificing taste or satisfaction. With easy-to-follow instructions and minimal prep time, these Crock-Pot dump meals make low-carb cooking accessible and enjoyable for everyone, from busy professionals to home cooks looking to simplify mealtime without compromising on flavor or nutrition.

Contents

Simple Soups and Stews 1
Spicy Pumpkin Chicken Soup 1
Monterey Corn Chowder 3
Mexican Crab Bisque 5
Easy Gumbo 7
Garlicky Chicken Stew 9
Chili Releno Soup 11
Three Cheese French Onion Soup 13
New Chicken Favorites 14
Parmesan Crab Stuffed Chicken 14
Marinated Thai Chicken 16
Cranberry Chicken 18
Elegant Mushroom Chicken 19
Maple Balsamic Chicken 21
Lemongrass Chicken with Zucchini Noodles 23
Smothered Chicken 25
Jerk Chicken with Greens 27
Chicken Fajita Casserole 29
Olive Chicken 31
Anise Blessed Chicken 33
Best Beef Dishes 34
Peppery Roast with Beets and Sprouts 34
Irish Corned Beef Dinner 36
Cajun Beef Tips 37
Flank Steak Pinwheels and Squash 38

Steak with Spiced Coconut Sauce	40
Deconstructed Cabbage Rolls	42
Poached Beef Tenderloin with Winter Vegetables	43
Beef Taco Pot	44
Super Simple Swiss Steak	46
Beef Sausage and Peppers	47
Perfect Pork, Veal and Lamb Dishes	48
Herb Garden Stuffed Pork Loin	48
Garlic Lamb Shanks	50
Pork Medallions with Fennel and Leek	52
Veal Shank with Anchovy Sauce	53
Chilied Spareribs	55
Chinese Pork Ribs	56
Vegetable Stuffed Pork Chops	57
Sweet and Spicy Peachy Pork	59
Peanut Pork	60
Rainy Day Bratwurst Pot	62
Curried Lamb	63
Variety of Vegetables	65
Mexican Mock Mac and Cheese	65
Creamy Cabbage Au Gratin	67
Rustic Squash Bake	69
Spaghetti Squash with Mushrooms and Peppers	70
Creamy Spinach and Artichoke Casserole	72
Slow Cooked Ratatouille	74
Green Bean and Mushroom Casserole	76

Simple Soups and Stews

So many times, people have an image of low carb eating that includes only red meats and cheeses. Nothing could be further from the truth. In this section, we introduce you to unique, flavorful soups and stews that will make sure that you will never be stuck in a rut of low carb options. With easy preparation, these soups and stews will provide enjoyable and warming nourishment to the body and soul.

Spicy Pumpkin Chicken Soup

Cook time 4-6 hours
Prep time 10 minutes
Serves 6

Ingredients
1 pound boneless, skinless chicken breasts, cubed
1 cup yellow onion, diced
1 cup celery, diced
3 cloves garlic, crushed and minced
1 cup red bell pepper, sliced
4 cups chicken stock
2 cups pureed pumpkin
2 teaspoons tarragon
½ teaspoon cayenne powder
½ teaspoon nutmeg
1 teaspoon salt
1 teaspoon white pepper
4 cups fresh spinach, torn

Directions

1. Set up and prepare your slow cooker.

2. Add the chicken, followed by the onion, celery, garlic, and bell pepper.
3. In a bowl, combine the chicken stock, pumpkin, tarragon, cayenne powder, nutmeg, and white pepper. Mix well and add to the slow cooker. Stir gently.
4. Cover and cook for 4 hours on HIGH or 6 hours on LOW.
5. Half an hour before the end of the cooking time, open the lid and mix in the spinach. Cook until the spinach is wilted and heated through.

Nutritional information
Calories 187
Total fat 4 g, saturated fat 1 g
Net carbohydrates 12 g
Protein 23 g

Monterey Corn Chowder

Cook Time: 4-6 hours
Prep Time: 10 minutes
Serves: 6

Ingredients:
1 pound boneless skinless chicken breast, cubed
1 red onion, diced
3 cloves garlic, crushed and minced
1 tablespoon jalapeno pepper, diced
1 cup red bell pepper, diced
1 cup fresh corn kernels
1 tablespoon olive oil
4 cups chicken stock
½ cup picante sauce
1 tablespoon ground cumin
2 teaspoons cayenne sauce
2 tablespoons cornstarch
1 cup milk (2%)
1 cup Monterey jack cheese, shredded
Fresh cilantro for garnish

Directions:
1. Set up and prepare your slow cooker.
2. Add the chicken, followed by the onion, garlic, jalapeno pepper, red bell pepper, and corn kernels.
3. Add the olive oil and toss lightly to coat.
4. Combine the chicken stock, picante sauce, cumin, cayenne sauce, and cornstarch. Whisk well until no lumps remain.
5. Add the stock mixture to the slow cooker.
6. Cover and cook for 4 hours on HIGH or 6 hours on LOW.

7. About half an hour before you are ready to eat, remove the lid and add the milk or heavy cream and Monterey jack cheese. Mix in before replacing the cover and continuing to cook.
8. Serve garnished with fresh cilantro, if desired.

Nutritional information:
Calories 273
Total fat 10 g, saturated fat 5 g
Net carbohydrates 14 g
Protein 28 g

Mexican Crab Bisque

Cook Time: 2 hours
Prep Time: 10 minutes
Serves: 4-6

Ingredients:
1 pound crab meat
1 cup yellow onion, diced
3 cloves garlic, crushed and minced
2 teaspoons chili powder
1 teaspoon cumin
1 teaspoon coriander
3 cups chicken or vegetable stock
1 cup milk or heavy cream
½ cup sour cream
Cubed avocado, for garnish if desired

Directions:

1. Set up and prepare your slow cooker.
2. Add the crab meat, onion and garlic.
3. Season with the chili powder, cumin, and coriander.
4. Add the chicken or vegetable stock.
5. Cover and cook for 2 hours on LOW.
6. About half an hour before you are ready to eat, remove the lid and add the milk or heavy cream and sour cream. Mix well before replacing the lid and continuing to cook.
7. Depending upon the desired texture of the soup, you can remove half of the soup and puree it in a blender before adding it back into the slow cooker. This will give your soup more of a bisque texture as opposed to a more rustic, chunkier texture.
8. Serve garnished with fresh avocado, if desired.

Nutritional information:
Calories 300
Total fat 11 g, saturated fat 5 g
Net carbohydrates 12 g
Protein 34 g

Easy Gumbo

Cook Time: 4 hours
Prep Time: 10 minutes
Serves: 4-6

Ingredients:
½ pound boneless skinless chicken breast, cubed
½ pound smoked ham, cubed
¼ cup peppered bacon, diced and lightly browned
½ cup yellow onion, diced
½ cup celery, diced
2 cloves garlic, crushed and minced
½ cup poblano pepper, diced
1 cup frozen okra, sliced
2 cups canned crushed tomatoes, including liquid
2 cups chicken stock
1 teaspoon cayenne powder
2 teaspoons cayenne pepper sauce
1 teaspoon salt
1 teaspoon black pepper

Directions:
1. Set up and prepare your slow cooker.
2. Add the chicken, followed by the ham, bacon, onion, celery, garlic, poblano peppers, and okra.
3. Next add the crushed tomatoes, including liquid, along with the chicken stock.
4. Season with cayenne powder, cayenne pepper sauce, salt, and black pepper.
5. Cover and cook on LOW for 4 hours.

Nutritional information:
Calories 251

Total fat 7 g, saturated fat 2 g
Net carbohydrates 8 g
Protein 32 g

Garlicky Chicken Stew

Cook Time: 4-6 hours
Prep Time: 10 minutes
Serves: 8

Ingredients:
2 pounds boneless chicken, both white and dark meats
1 cup red onion, sliced
2 cups sweet potatoes, cubed
2 cups mini portabella mushrooms, halved
1 cup celery, diced
6 cloves garlic, crushed and minced
1 sprig fresh rosemary
2 bay leaves
1 teaspoon salt
1 teaspoon black pepper
4 cups chicken stock
2 tablespoons soy sauce
1 tablespoon cornstarch

Directions:

1. Set up and prepare your slow cooker.
2. Add the chicken, followed by the red onion, sweet potatoes, mini portabella mushrooms, celery, and garlic.
3. Season with the rosemary, bay leaves, salt, and black pepper.
4. In a bowl, combine the chicken stock, soy sauce, and cornstarch. Mix with a whisk until no lumps remain.
5. Add the broth to the slow cooker.
6. Cover and cook for 4 hours on HIGH or 6 hours on LOW.

Nutritional information:
Calories 130

Total fat 2 g, saturated fat 1 g
Net carbohydrates 15 g
Protein 10 g

Chili Releno Soup

Cook Time: 4-6 hours
Prep Time: 10 minutes
Serves: 4-6

Ingredients:
1 pound beef stew meat
1 cup red onion, diced
3 cups canned stewed tomatoes, with liquid
4 cloves garlic, crushed and minced
2 cups poblano peppers, seeded and chopped
2 cups beef stock
1 tablespoon chili powder
1 teaspoon cinnamon
¼ cup fresh cilantro, chopped
1 cup Cotija cheese, crumbled
Diced avocado for garnish
Additional cilantro for garnish

Directions:

1. Set up and prepare your slow cooker.
2. Add the stew meat, followed by the red onion, stewed tomatoes and liquid, garlic, and poblano peppers.
3. Combine the beef stock with the chili powder, cinnamon, and cilantro. Mix and add to the slow cooker.
4. Cover and cook for 4 hours on HIGH or 6 hours on LOW.
5. About half an hour before you are ready to eat, remove the lid and add the Cotija cheese. Mix well before replacing the cover and continuing to cook.
6. Serve garnished with avocado and fresh cilantro, if desired.

Nutritional information:

Calories 283
Total fat 11 g, saturated fat 6 g
Net carbohydrates 8 g
Protein 30 g

Three Cheese French Onion Soup

Cook Time: 4 hours
Prep Time: 15 minutes
Serves: 6

Ingredients:
6 cups sweet yellow onions, thinly sliced
1 tablespoon olive oil
1 sprig fresh rosemary
1 tablespoon fresh thyme
6 cups beef stock
½ cup Swiss cheese, shredded
½ cup Brie cheese, sliced thick
½ cup fresh grated Parmesan cheese

Directions:

1. Set up and prepare your slow cooker.
2. Add the onions, followed by the olive oil, rosemary, and thyme. Toss to mix.
3. Add the beef stock, cover and cook on LOW for 4 hours.
4. Preheat the broiler of your oven, and ladle the soup into heat proof bowls.
5. Layer on a piece of Brie cheese, followed by some Swiss and Parmesan cheese.
6. Place under the broiler for 2-3 minutes, or until cheese melts and caramelizes lightly.

Nutritional information:
Calories 207
Total fat 11 g, saturated fat 6 g
Net carbohydrates 11 g
Protein 15 g

New Chicken Favorites

Chicken is one of the favorite protein choices for the low carb lifestyle. It is lean, easy to prepare and extremely versatile, lending itself to an endless variety of dishes. In this section we have taken flavors both classic and new, and modified them to be created in just a few simple steps with your slow cooker.

Parmesan Crab Stuffed Chicken

Cook Time: 6 hours
Prep Time: 15 minutes
Serves: 4

Ingredients:
4 boneless, skinless chicken breasts, butterflied and pounded thin
½ pound crab meat
1 tablespoon shallots, chopped
1 teaspoon lemon zest
3 cups spaghetti squash (insides only)
1 teaspoon rubbed sage
1 teaspoon tarragon
1 cup chicken stock
2 tablespoons butter, diced
1 cup fresh spinach, torn
½ cup fresh grated Parmesan cheese

Directions:

1. Set up and prepare your slow cooker.
2. In a bowl, combine the crab meat, shallots, and lemon zest.
3. Spread equal amounts of the mixture in the center of each chicken breast.

4. Roll the chicken into a pinwheel and secure with cooking twine. Set aside.
5. In another bowl, combine the spaghetti squash, rubbed sage, tarragon, and butter.
6. Place the chicken into the slow cooker.
7. Arrange the spaghetti squash around and over the chicken, and pour the chicken stock around it.
8. Cover and cook for 6 hours on LOW.
9. In the final 30 minutes of cooking, stir in the spinach and Parmesan. Cook until the spinach is wilted, and the Parmesan is melted.

Nutritional information:
Calories 513
Total fat 18 g, saturated fat 8 g
Net carbohydrates 9 g
Protein 74 g

Marinated Thai Chicken

Cook Time: 4-6 hours
Prep Time: 10 minutes plus marinating time
Serves: 4

Ingredients:
1 pound boneless skinless chicken breast, sliced into strips
¼ cup soy sauce
2 teaspoons lime juice
¼ cup fresh basil, chopped
1 teaspoon fresh ginger, grated
¼ cup plain yogurt
1 cup yellow onion, sliced
2 cups assorted mushrooms, sliced
2 cups zucchini, sliced
2 cups asparagus, cut into 1-inch pieces
1 cup chicken stock
2 teaspoons sesame oil
Sesame seeds for garnish

Directions:

1. Set up and prepare your slow cooker.
2. In a bowl, combine the soy sauce, lime juice, basil, ginger, and yogurt.
3. Toss the chicken into the sauce mixture to coat. You can either place in the refrigerator to marinate for up to 8 hours, or you can immediately add the chicken to the slow cooker and proceed with the recipe instructions.
4. Add the onion, mushrooms, zucchini, and asparagus.
5. Combine the chicken stock with the sesame oil and add to the slow cooker.
6. Cover and cook for 4 hours on HIGH, or 6 hours on LOW.

7. Serve garnished with sesame seeds, if desired.

Nutritional information:
Calories 263
Total fat 7 g, saturated fat 2 g
Net carbohydrates 11 g
Protein 33 g

Cranberry Chicken

Cook Time: 6 hours
Prep Time: 10 minutes
Serves: 6-8

Ingredients:
2 pounds bone-in chicken pieces, skins removed
3 cups sweet potatoes, cubed
1 cup cranberries
1 tablespoon shallots
½ cup celery, diced
½ cup walnuts, chopped
½ cup apple cider
½ cup chicken stock
1 tablespoon apple cider vinegar
1 teaspoon stone ground mustard
1 teaspoon cinnamon
½ teaspoon ground cloves

Directions:

1. Set up and prepare your slow cooker.
2. Add the chicken to the slow cooker, followed by the sweet potatoes, cranberries, shallots, celery, and walnuts.
3. In a bowl, combine the apple cider, chicken stock, apple cider vinegar, mustard, cinnamon, and cloves. Pour over the chicken and vegetables.
4. Cover and cook for 6 hours on LOW.

Nutritional information:
Calories 146
Total fat 6 g, saturated fat 1 g
Net carbohydrates 13 g
Protein 8 g

Elegant Mushroom Chicken

Cook Time: 4-6 hours
Prep Time: 10 minutes
Serves: 4

Ingredients:
1 pound boneless skinless chicken breast
2 cups button mushrooms, sliced
1 cup red onion, diced
2 tablespoons olive oil
½ cup chicken stock
¼ cup semi sweet white wine
¼ cup heavy cream
2 teaspoons ground sage
1 teaspoon thyme
1 teaspoon salt
1 teaspoon pepper
Fresh salad greens or zucchini noodles for serving

Directions:

1. Set up and prepare your slow cooker.
2. Add the chicken to the slow cooker, followed by the mushrooms, red onion, and olive oil. Toss to mix.
3. In a bowl, combine the chicken stock, white wine, heavy cream, ground sage, thyme, salt, and pepper. Mix well and add to the slow cooker.
4. Cover and cook for 4 hours on HIGH or 6 hours on LOW.
5. Serve with fresh salad greens or zucchini noodles.

Nutritional information:
Calories 292
Total fat 16 g, saturated fat 5 g
Net carbohydrates 5 g

Protein 28 g

Maple Balsamic Chicken

Cook Time: 6 hours
Prep Time: 10 minutes
Serves: 6

Ingredients:
2 pounds bone-in chicken pieces, skins removed
1 tablespoon olive oil
1 cup red onion, sliced
2 cups acorn squash, peeled and sliced
2 cups fresh green beans, trimmed
2 cloves garlic, crushed and minced
1 cup chicken stock
¼ cup balsamic vinegar
1 tablespoon maple syrup
¼ cup fresh basil, chopped
1 tablespoon fresh thyme, chopped
1 teaspoon salt
1 teaspoon coarse ground black pepper
¼ cup goat cheese

Directions:

1. Set up and prepare your slow cooker.
2. Place the chicken and the olive oil to the slow cooker. Toss to coat.
3. Add the red onion, acorn squash, green beans, and garlic.
4. In a bowl, combine the chicken stock, balsamic vinegar, and maple syrup. Mix well and add to the slow cooker.
5. Season with the basil, thyme, salt, and black pepper.
6. Cover and cook for 6 hours on LOW.
7. About half an hour before you are ready to eat, remove the lid and gently stir in the goat cheese. Replace the

cover and continue to cook.

Nutritional information:
Calories 172
Total fat 8 g, saturated fat 2 g
Net carbohydrates 12 g
Protein 11 g

Lemongrass Chicken with Zucchini Noodles

Cook Time: 4 hours
Prep Time: 15 minutes
Serves: 4

Ingredients:
1 pound boneless skinless chicken breast, sliced into strips
1 tablespoon olive oil
½ cup ponzu or soy sauce
2 teaspoons fresh ginger, grated
2 cloves garlic, crushed and minced
1 tablespoon fresh lemongrass, chopped
1 tablespoon crushed red pepper flakes
4 cups zucchini noodles (fresh zucchini sliced into thin, noodle-like strips)
1 cup carrots, peeled and thinly sliced
2 teaspoons sesame oil
1 teaspoon black pepper
1 cup coconut milk
Chopped peanuts for garnish, if desired

Directions:
1. Set up and prepare your slow cooker.
2. Arrange the chicken strips in the slow cooker.
3. In a bowl, combine the olive oil, ponzu or soy sauce, ginger, garlic, lemongrass, and crushed red pepper flakes. Mix well and pour over the chicken.
4. Next add the zucchini noodles and carrots.
5. Season with sesame oil and black pepper.
6. Add the coconut milk, and then cover and cook for 4 hours on LOW.
7. *Serve garnished with chopped peanuts, if desired.*

Nutritional information:
Calories 341
Total fat 19 g, saturated fat 11 g
Net carbohydrates 10 g
Protein 29 g

Smothered Chicken

Cook Time: 6 hours
Prep Time: 10 minutes
Serves: 6

Ingredients:
1 pound boneless skinless chicken breasts
1 cup sweet yellow onion, sliced
2 cups cremini mushrooms, halved
2 cups butternut squash, peeled and cubed
2 cloves garlic, crushed and minced
1 teaspoon ground sage
1 teaspoon thyme
½ teaspoon nutmeg
1 teaspoon salt
1 teaspoon black pepper
1 cup chicken stock
½ cup heavy cream
½ cup cream cheese, cubed
½ cup Swiss cheese, shredded
¼ cup chives, chopped

Directions:
1. Set up and prepare your slow cooker.
2. Add the chicken to the slow cooker followed by the onion, cremini mushrooms, butternut squash, and garlic.
3. Season with the ground sage, thyme, nutmeg, salt, and black pepper.
4. Add the chicken stock and cover to cook for 6 hours on LOW.
5. About half an hour before you are ready to eat, add the heavy cream, cream cheese, Swiss cheese, and chives.

Mix before replacing the lid and continuing to cook.

Nutritional information:
Calories 318
Total fat 19 g, saturated fat 11 g
Net carbohydrates 11 g
Protein 24 g

Jerk Chicken with Greens

Cook Time: 6 hours
Prep Time: 10 minutes
Serves: 8

Ingredients:
2 pounds bone-in chicken pieces, skin removed
1 teaspoon cinnamon
½ teaspoon nutmeg
¼ teaspoon ground cloves
1 teaspoon salt
1 teaspoon black pepper
1 cup sweet yellow onion, sliced
3 cloves garlic, crushed and minced
2 cups sweet potatoes, cubed
4 cups fresh greens, such as collard greens
1 cup fresh pineapple chunks
1 tablespoon jalapeno pepper, diced
1 cup chicken stock
½ cup unsweetened apple juice
1 teaspoon lime juice

Directions:

1. Set up and prepare your slow cooker.
2. Add the chicken and season with cinnamon, nutmeg, cloves, salt, and black pepper.
3. Next, add the onion, garlic, sweet potatoes, pineapple chunks, and jalapeno pepper.
4. Cover with chicken stock, apple juice, and lime juice.
5. Cover and cook for 6 hours on LOW.
6. About half an hour before you are ready to eat, add the greens and stir to mix. Serve when wilted and warmed

through.

Nutritional information:
Calories 115
Total fat 1 g, saturated fat 0 g
Net carbohydrates 14 g
Protein 8 g

Chicken Fajita Casserole

Cook Time: 4 hours
Prep Time: 10 minutes
Serves: 4-6

Ingredients:
1 pound boneless skinless chicken breast, cut into strips
2 teaspoons cumin
2 cloves garlic, crushed and minced
1 cup red onion, sliced
4 cups cauliflower florets
1 cup green bell pepper, sliced
1 cup red bell pepper, sliced
1 cup tomatoes, diced
1 ½ cups chicken stock
1 teaspoon chili powder
1 teaspoon paprika
½ teaspoon cinnamon
1 teaspoon salt
1 teaspoon black pepper
2 teaspoons lime juice
1 cup Cotija cheese, crumbled
½ cup cream cheese, cubed
Avocado for garnish if desired, sliced

Directions:

1. Set up and prepare your slow cooker.
2. Add the chicken breast and season with cumin before adding the garlic, red onion, cauliflower, green bell pepper, red bell pepper, and tomatoes.
3. Combine the chicken stock with the chili powder, paprika, cinnamon, salt, black pepper, and lime juice. Add to the

slow cooker.
4. Cover and cook for 4 hours on LOW.
5. About half an hour before you are ready to eat, remove the lid and add the Cotija cheese and cream cheese. Mix well before replacing the lid and continuing to cook.
6. Serve garnished with fresh avocado, if desired.

Nutritional information:
Calories 491
Total fat 29 g, saturated fat 16 g
Net carbohydrates 14 g
Protein 45 g

Olive Chicken

Cook Time: 6 hours
Prep Time: 10 minutes
Serves: 4-6

Ingredients:
2 pounds bone-in chicken pieces, skin removed
1 cup pearl onions, peeled
3 cloves garlic, crushed and minced
2 cups carrots, peeled and sliced
3 cups Brussels sprouts, halved
1 cup large green olives, pitted and halved
½ cup dry white wine
1 cup chicken stock
2 sprigs fresh rosemary
1 tablespoon fresh oregano
1 teaspoon salt
1 teaspoon black pepper

Directions:
1. Set up and prepare the slow cooker.
2. Arrange the chicken in the slow cooker, followed by the pearl onions, garlic, carrots, Brussels sprouts, and green olives.
3. Combine the dry white wine with the chicken stock and add to the slow cooker.
4. Season with rosemary, oregano, salt, and black pepper.
5. Cover and cook for 6 hours on LOW.

Nutritional information:
Calories 252
Total fat 10 g, saturated fat 1 g
Net carbohydrates 13 g

Protein 15 g

Anise Blessed Chicken

Cook Time: 8 hours
Prep Time: 10 minutes
Serves: 4-6

Ingredients:
4-5 pound whole chicken
2 bay leaves
¼ cup fresh parsley
1 tablespoon fresh thyme
1 tablespoon caraway seeds
4 star anise
2 cups chicken stock
2 cups carrots, peeled and sliced
2 cups yellow squash, peeled and diced

Directions:

1. Set up and prepare your slow cooker.
2. Place the chicken in the slow cooker and season with bay leaves, parsley, thyme, caraway seeds, and star anise.
3. Add the chicken stock, carrots, and yellow squash.
4. Cover and cook for 8 hours on LOW.

Nutritional information:
Calories 198
Total fat 5 g, saturated fat 1 g
Net carbohydrates 10 g
Protein 25 g

Best Beef Dishes

Beef is rich and decadent, and a low carb lifestyle staple. The only problem with beef is that we tend to limit ourselves in the ways that we prepare it, and the flavors that we combine with it. With the help of your slow cooker, you can expand your flavor horizons and explore new tastes and textures with your beef dishes, such as the ones included in these recipes.

Peppery Roast with Beets and Sprouts

Cook Time: 8 hours
Prep Time: 10 minutes
Serves: 8

Ingredients:
1 3-4 pound beef roast
2 tablespoons coarse ground mustard
1 tablespoon coarse ground black pepper
3 cloves garlic, crushed and minced
1 teaspoon salt
2 cups beets, sliced
3 cups Brussels sprouts, chopped
1 tablespoon olive oil
1 tablespoon fresh mint

Directions:

1. Set up and prepare your slow cooker.
2. Season the roast with coarse ground mustard, black pepper, garlic, and salt before adding it to the slow cooker.
3. Next, add the beets and Brussels sprouts.
4. Drizzle with olive oil and season with fresh mint.

5. Cover and cook for 8 hours on LOW or until roast has reached desired doneness.

Nutritional information:
Calories 553
Total fat 35 g, saturated fat 3 g
Net carbohydrates 4 g
Protein 50 g

Irish Corned Beef Dinner

Cook Time: 6-8 hours
Prep Time: 10 minutes
Serves: 8

Ingredients:
1 3-4 pound beef brisket
1 tablespoon pickling spice
1 teaspoon ground caraway seeds
3 cups cabbage, chopped
2 cups carrots, peeled and sliced
2 cup turnips, peeled and sliced
3 cups beef stock
½ cup dark beer

Directions:
1. Set up and prepare your slow cooker.
2. Season the brisket with the pickling spice and caraway seeds before placing it in the slow cooker.
3. Add the cabbage, carrots, turnips, beef stock and dark beer.
4. Cover and cook for 6 hours on HIGH or 8 hours on LOW.

Nutritional information:
Calories 264
Total fat 7 g, saturated fat 2 g
Net carbohydrates 6 g
Protein 40 g

Cajun Beef Tips

Cook Time: 4-6 hours
Prep Time: 10 minutes
Serves: 6

Ingredients:
2 pounds sirloin beef tips
1 cup celery, diced
1 cup red onion, sliced
1 cup red bell pepper, sliced
2 cloves garlic, crushed and minced
½ cup poblano pepper, diced
2 cups canned stewed tomatoes
1 cup beef stock
2 tablespoons Cajun seasoning
1 teaspoon salt
1 teaspoon black pepper

Directions:

1. Set up and prepare your slow cooker.
2. Add the beef tips, followed by the celery, red onion, red bell pepper, garlic, poblano pepper, and stewed tomatoes.
3. Add the beef stock and Cajun seasoning, salt, and black pepper.
4. Cover and cook for 4 hours on HIGH or 6 hours on LOW.

Nutritional information:
Calories 394
Total fat 24 g, saturated fat 9 g
Total carbohydrates 8 g
Protein 31 g

Flank Steak Pinwheels and Squash

Cook Time: 8 hours
Prep Time: 15 minutes
Serves: 4-6

Ingredients:
1 pound beef flank steak
2 tablespoons olive oil
½ cup bacon, cooked and crumbled
2 cloves garlic, crushed and minced
1 cup tomatoes, diced
¼ cup fresh parsley, chopped
½ cup yellow onion, diced
¼ cup fresh basil, chopped
2 cups butternut squash, peeled and cubed
2 cups cremini mushrooms, halved
2 tablespoons Worcestershire sauce
1 tablespoon balsamic vinegar
1 cup beef stock
4 cups fresh spinach, torn

Directions:

1. Set up and prepare your slow cooker.
2. Arrange the flank steak in the slow cooker and drizzle with olive oil.
3. Add the bacon, garlic, tomatoes, parsley, yellow onion, basil, butternut squash, and cremini mushrooms.
4. In a bowl, combine the Worcestershire sauce, balsamic vinegar, and beef stock, and add to the slow cooker.
5. Cover and cook for 8 hours on LOW.
6. About half an hour before you are ready to eat, stir in the spinach and cook until wilted and heated through.

Nutritional information:
Calories 330
Total fat 16 g, saturated fat 5 g
Net carbohydrates 14 g
Protein 29 g

Steak with Spiced Coconut Sauce

Cook Time: 4-6 hours
Prep Time: 10 minutes
Serves: 4-6

Ingredients:
1 pound flank steak, sliced into strips
1 cup red onion, sliced
4 cups cauliflower florets
1 cup chickpeas, canned or cooked
1 tablespoon olive oil
2 cups beef stock
2 cups unsweetened coconut milk
½ cup shredded unsweetened coconut
1 tablespoon tomato paste
1 tablespoon lime juice
3 tablespoons soy sauce
4 cloves garlic, crushed and minced
1 tablespoon fresh grated ginger
1 teaspoon cinnamon
1 teaspoon coriander

Directions:

1. Set up and prepare your slow cooker.
2. Arrange the flank steak in the slow cooker, and layer on the red onion, cauliflower, chickpeas, and olive oil.
3. In a bowl, combine the beef stock, unsweetened coconut milk, shredded coconut, tomato paste, lime juice, soy sauce, garlic, ginger, cinnamon, and coriander. Mix well before adding to the slow cooker.
4. Cover and cook for 4 hours on HIGH or 6 hours on LOW.

Nutritional information:

Calories 370
Total fat 23 g, saturated fat 15 g
Net carbohydrates 15 g
Protein 22 g

Deconstructed Cabbage Rolls

Cook Time: 6 hours
Prep Time: 10 minutes
Serves: 6

Ingredients:
1 pound lean ground beef
½ cup bacon, cooked and crumbled
4 cups cabbage, sliced
1 cup yellow onion, diced
2 cups stewed tomatoes, with liquid
2 cloves garlic, crushed and minced
1 cup beef stock
¼ cup apple cider vinegar
½ teaspoon cinnamon
2 teaspoons caraway seeds
1 teaspoon salt
1 teaspoon black pepper

Directions:
1. Set up and prepare your slow cooker.
2. Add the ground beef, bacon, cabbage, yellow onion, stewed tomatoes, and garlic.
3. In a bowl, combine the beef stock, apple cider vinegar, cinnamon, caraway, salt, and black pepper. Mix well before adding to the slow cooker.
4. Cover and cook for 6 hours on LOW.

Nutritional information:
Calories 247
Total fat 16 g, saturated fat 6 g
Net carbohydrates 6 g
Protein 16 g

Poached Beef Tenderloin with Winter Vegetables

Cook Time: 8 hours
Prep Time: 10 minutes
Serves: 6

Ingredients:
2 pounds beef tenderloin roast
1 teaspoon salt
1 teaspoon black pepper
1 sprig fresh rosemary
1 tablespoon fresh thyme
3 cups beef stock
2 cups carrots, peeled and sliced thick
2 cups beets, peeled and sliced
2 cups parsnips, peeled and sliced

Directions:

1. Set up and prepare your slow cooker.
2. Arrange the beef tenderloin in the slow cooker and season with salt, black pepper, rosemary, and thyme.
3. Cover with beef stock and then add the carrots, beets, and parsnips.
4. Cover and cook on LOW for 8 hours.

Nutritional information:
Calories 466
Total fat 28 g, saturated fat 11 g
Net carbohydrates 14 g
Protein 33 g

Beef Taco Pot

Cook Time: 6 hours
Prep Time: 10 minutes
Serves: 4

Ingredients:
1 pound lean ground beef
1 cup red onion, diced
1 cup green bell pepper, diced
1 cup fresh corn kernels
1 cup tomatoes, chopped
1 cup poblano pepper, diced
½ cup black olives, sliced
1 tablespoon ground cumin
2 teaspoons chili powder
1 teaspoon garlic powder
1 teaspoon cayenne powder
1 teaspoon black pepper
1 teaspoon salt
½ cup beef stock or tomato juice
½ cup Cotija cheese, crumbled

Directions:

1. Set up and prepare your slow cooker.
2. Add the ground beef, red onion, green bell pepper, fresh corn kernels, tomatoes, poblano pepper and black olives.
3. Season with cumin, chili powder, garlic powder, cayenne powder, black pepper and salt.
4. Add the beef stock or tomato juice, cover and cook for 6 hours on LOW.
5. About half an hour before you are ready to eat remove the cover and add the Cotija cheese. Replace the lid and

continue cooking.

Nutritional information:
Calories 463
Total fat 32 g, saturated fat 14 g
Net carbohydrates 14 g
Protein 29 g

Super Simple Swiss Steak

Cook Time: 4-6 hours
Prep Time: 10 minutes
Serves: 2-3

Ingredients:
1 pound sirloin steak, cubed
1 teaspoon salt
1 teaspoon black pepper
3 cloves garlic, crushed and minced
1 cup celery, chopped
1 cup carrots, chopped
1 cup yellow onion, sliced
2 cups canned tomatoes, with liquid
1 ½ cups beef stock
1 teaspoon tarragon

Directions:
1. Set up and prepare your slow cooker.
2. Season the steak with salt and black pepper, and arrange it in the slow cooker. Add the garlic, celery, carrots, yellow onion, and canned tomatoes (including liquid) to the slow cooker.
3. Cover with the beef stock and season with tarragon.
4. Cover and cook for 4 hours on HIGH or 6 hours on LOW, or until meat has reached desired doneness.

Nutritional information:
Calories 211
Total fat 5 g, saturated fat 2 g
Net carbohydrates 10 g
Protein 29 g

Beef Sausage and Peppers

Cook Time: 4-6 hours
Prep Time: 10 minutes
Serves: 4

Ingredients:
1 pound beef sausage links, cut into thick slices
1 cup yellow onion, sliced
1 cup red bell pepper, sliced
2 cups green bell pepper, sliced
1 cup cherry tomatoes, halved
1 cup beef stock
2 teaspoons tomato paste
½ cup fresh basil, chopped
1 tablespoon fresh oregano
1 teaspoon salt
1 teaspoon black pepper

Directions:

1. Set up and prepare your slow cooker.
2. Add the beef sausage to the slow cooker, followed by the yellow onion, red bell pepper, green bell pepper and cherry tomatoes.
3. In a bowl combine the beef stock, tomato paste, fresh basil, oregano, salt and black pepper.
4. Cover and cook for 4 hours on HIGH or 6 hours on LOW.

Nutritional information:
Calories 268
Total fat 20 g, saturated fat 7 g
Net carbohydrates 10 g
Protein 11 g

Perfect Pork, Veal and Lamb Dishes

When you are looking for something a little different, whether it be for company or just to expand your own dinner options, pork, veal, and lamb offer new choices in flavors and textures. There is no reason to shy away from these meats when using your slow cooker. They cook up beautifully tender, providing you with savory, delicious meals.

Herb Garden Stuffed Pork Loin

Cook Time: 8 hours
Prep Time: 15 minutes
Serves: 8

Ingredients:
3 pound pork tenderloin roast
¼ cup stone ground mustard
4 cloves garlic, crushed and minced
1 teaspoon black pepper
4 tablespoons butter
¼ cup fresh basil, chopped
¼ cup fresh chives, chopped
¼ cup fresh sage, chopped
2 cups cherry tomatoes, halved
2 cups fresh spinach
1 cup chicken or vegetable stock

Directions:
1. Prepare and set up your slow cooker.
2. Slice the tenderloin ¾ of the way through along one side and spread it open.

3. In a bowl, combine the butter, basil, chives, and sage. Mix well and spread along the inside of the pork.
4. Fold the pork back over, securing with cooking twine, if needed.
5. Season the pork with stone ground mustard, garlic, and black pepper. Place in the slow cooker.
6. Add the tomatoes, chicken or vegetable stock.
7. Cover and cook for 8 hours on LOW.
8. About half an hour before you are ready to eat, open the lid and stir in the spinach. Serve when the spinach is wilted and the meat is cooked through.

Nutritional information:
Calories 418
Total fat 20 g, saturated fat 7 g
Net carbohydrates 3 g
Protein 52 g

Garlic Lamb Shanks

Cook Time: 6-8 hours
Prep Time: 10 minutes
Serves: 4-6

Ingredients:
2 pound lamb shank
5 whole cloves garlic
1 tablespoon olive oil
1 cup carrots, peeled and diced
1 cup celery, diced
1 cup onion, diced
2 cups rutabaga, peeled and cubed
2 cups Swiss chard, torn
2 cups vegetable stock
2 teaspoons tomato paste
1 teaspoon honey
¼ cup dry red wine
¼ cup fresh parsley, chopped
1 tablespoon fresh thyme, chopped
1 tablespoon black peppercorns

Directions:

1. Set up and prepare your slow cooker.
2. Add the lamb to the slow cooker, together with the garlic cloves.
3. Drizzle with olive oil.
4. Add the carrots, celery, onion, and rutabaga.
5. In a bowl, combine the vegetable stock, tomato paste, honey, dry red wine, parsley, thyme and black peppercorns.
6. Pour the stock mixture over the lamb and vegetables.

7. Cover and cook on HIGH for 6 hours, or on LOW for 8 hours.

Nutritional information:
Calories 282
Total fat 9 g, saturated fat 3 g
Net carbohydrates 11 g
Protein 33 g

Pork Medallions with Fennel and Leek

Cook Time: 8 hours
Prep Time: 10 minutes
Serves: 6

Ingredients:
2 pounds pork medallions
3 cloves garlic, crushed and minced
1 tablespoon olive oil
1 cup vegetable or chicken stock
1 cup leeks, sliced
2 cups fennel bulbs, sliced
1 sprig fresh rosemary
1 teaspoon salt
1 teaspoon black pepper

Directions:

1. Set up and prepare your slow cooker.
2. Arrange the pork and the garlic in the slow cooker.
3. Drizzle with olive oil before adding the vegetable stock.
4. Add the leeks, fennel, rosemary, salt, and black pepper.
5. Cover and cook for 8 hours on LOW.

Nutritional information:
Calories 356
Total fat 15 g, saturated fat 4 g
Net carbohydrates 4 g
Protein 46 g

Veal Shank with Anchovy Sauce

Cook Time: 8 hours
Prep Time: 15 minutes
Serves: 6

Ingredients:
2 pounds veal shank cross cuts
1 cup onion, sliced
1 cup carrot, sliced
½ cup celery, diced
1 cup chicken or vegetable stock
½ cup dry white wine
¼ cup fresh parsley, chopped
1 tablespoon fresh thyme
1 teaspoon tomato paste
½ teaspoon salt
1 teaspoon black pepper

Sauce
2 cloves garlic, crushed and minced
1 teaspoon lemon zest
¼ cup fresh parsley, chopped
1 tablespoon anchovy, chopped
1 tablespoon olive oil

Directions:

1. Set up and prepare your slow cooker.
2. Place the veal in the slow cooker followed by the onion, carrot, and celery.
3. Add the chicken or vegetable stock, tomato paste, and the dry white wine.
4. Season with parsley, thyme, salt, and black pepper.
5. Cover and cook for 8 hours on LOW.

6. To make the sauce: Combine the garlic, lemon zest, parsley, anchovy, and olive oil in a blender or food processer. Pulse until smooth and serve on the side with the veal.

Nutritional information:
Calories 348
Total fat 10 g, saturated fat 2 g
Net carbohydrates 5 g
Protein 52 g

Chilied Spareribs

Cook Time: 8 hours
Prep Time: 10 minutes
Serves: 4

Ingredients:
2-3 pounds pork spareribs
2 tablespoons brown sugar
1 tablespoon chili powder
1 teaspoon cayenne powder
2 tablespoons paprika
1 teaspoon onion powder
1 teaspoon salt
1 teaspoon black pepper
2 cups yellow onion, sliced
½-1 cup chicken or vegetable stock

Directions:
1. Set up and prepare your slow cooker.
2. In a bowl, combine the brown sugar, chili powder, cayenne powder, paprika, onion powder, salt, and black pepper. Rub the mixture into the spareribs.
3. Place the spareribs in the slow cooker.
4. Cover with the yellow onion and add the vegetable stock.
5. Cover and cook for 8 hours on LOW.

Nutritional information:
Calories 484
Total fat 35 g, saturated fat 13 g
Net carbohydrates 7 g
Protein 34 g

Chinese Pork Ribs

Cook Time: 8 hours
Prep Time: 10 minutes
Serves: 4

Ingredients:
2-3 pounds pork spareribs
3 cloves garlic, crushed and minced
¼ cup soy sauce
2 tablespoons low sugar orange marmalade
3 tablespoons ketchup
3 cups bok choy, chopped
1 cup chicken or vegetable stock

Directions:

1. Set up and prepare your slow cooker.
2. In a bowl combine the soy sauce, orange marmalade and ketchup. Mix well and brush over the spareribs.
3. Place the spareribs in the slow cooker along with the garlic.
4. Add the chicken or vegetable stock.
5. Cover and cook for 8 hours on LOW.
6. About half an hour before you are ready to eat, open the lid and stir in the bok choy. Serve when the greens are wilted and the meat is tender.

Nutritional information:
Calories 482
Total fat 35 g, saturated fat 13 g
Net carbohydrates 6 g
Protein 35 g

Vegetable Stuffed Pork Chops

Cook Time: 8 hours
Prep Time: 15 minutes
Serves: 4

Ingredients:

4 bone-in pork chops
¼ cup yellow onion, diced
¼ cup red bell pepper, diced
½ cup fresh corn kernels
½ cup poblano pepper, diced
4 cups asparagus spears, cut into 1-inch pieces
1 cup chicken or vegetable stock
1 teaspoon cumin
1 teaspoon garlic powder
1 teaspoon salt
1 teaspoon black pepper

Directions:

1. Set up and prepare your slow cooker.
2. Cut the pork chops along the side, going about ¾ of the way into the meat.
3. In a bowl, combine the onion, red bell pepper, corn, and poblano peppers. Mix well and spoon the mixture into the center of each pork chop.
4. Season the pork chops with cumin, garlic powder, salt, and pepper before adding to the slow cooker.
5. Add the chicken or vegetable stock.
6. Cover and cook for 8 hours on LOW.
7. About half an hour before you are ready to eat, add the asparagus. Serve when the asparagus is tender and the meat is cooked through.

Nutritional information:
Calories 221
Total fat 7 g, saturated fat 3 g
Net carbohydrates 9 g
Protein 26 g

Sweet and Spicy Peachy Pork

Cook Time: 4-6 hours
Prep Time: 10 minutes
Serves: 4

Ingredients:
4 bone-in pork chops
¼ teaspoon cinnamon
¼ teaspoon cloves
1 tablespoon crushed red pepper flakes
1 cup sweet yellow onion, sliced
2 cups fresh peaches, sliced
1 cup chicken or vegetable stock
1 tablespoon lemon juice
2 tablespoons orange juice

Directions:

1. Set up and prepare your slow cooker.
2. Season the pork chops with the cinnamon, cloves, and crushed red pepper flakes before placing them in the slow cooker.
3. Add the onion and peaches.
4. In a bowl, combine the chicken or vegetable stock, lemon juice, and orange juice. Mix well and add to the slow cooker.
5. Cover and cook for 4 hours on HIGH, or 6 hours on LOW.

Nutritional information:
Calories 217
Total fat 7 g, saturated fat 3 g
Net carbohydrates 12 g
Protein 24 g

Peanut Pork

Cook Time: 4-6 hours
Prep Time: 10 minutes
Serves: 4-6

Ingredients:
1 pound pork, cut into slices
1 cup yellow onion, sliced
3 cups broccoli florets
1 cup chicken or vegetable stock
¼ cup sugar free creamy peanut butter
2 tablespoons soy sauce
1 tablespoon lemon juice
1 teaspoon chili powder
1 teaspoon salt
1 teaspoon black pepper
1 cup peanuts, chopped

Directions:
1. Set up and prepare your slow cooker.
2. Arrange the pork in the slow cooker, followed by the onion. If possible, keep the broccoli out until the final hour of cooking. Otherwise, add it as well.
3. In a bowl, combine the chicken or vegetable stock, peanut butter, soy sauce, lemon juice, chili powder, salt, and black pepper. Mix well and add to the slow cooker.
4. Add the peanuts.
5. Cover and cook for 4 hours on HIGH or 6 hours on LOW.

Nutritional information:
Calories 461
Total fat 28 g, saturated fat 5 g
Net carbohydrates 11 g

Protein 39 g

Rainy Day Bratwurst Pot

Cook Time: 4-6 hours
Prep Time: 10 minutes
Serves: 4

Ingredients:
1 pound bratwurst links, sliced thick
2 cups carrots, peeled and sliced
1 cup celery, sliced
1 cup red onion, diced
4 cups cabbage, sliced
2 cups chicken or vegetable stock
1 cup stewed tomatoes, with liquid
1 teaspoon thyme
1 teaspoon basil
1 teaspoon salt
1 teaspoon black pepper

Directions:
1. Set up and prepare your slow cooker.
2. Add the bratwurst along with the carrots, celery, red onion and cabbage.
3. Next add in the chicken or vegetable stock and the stewed tomatoes with the liquid.
4. Season with thyme, basil, salt and black pepper.
5. Cover and cook for 4 hours on HIGH, or 6 hours on LOW.

Nutritional information:
Calories 336
Total fat 23 g, saturated fat 8 g
Net carbohydrates 14 g
Protein 14 g

Curried Lamb

Cook Time: 4-6 hours
Prep Time: 10 minutes
Serves: 4

Ingredients:
1 pound lamb, cut into strips
1 cup apple, chopped
1 cup green bell pepper
½ cup celery, diced
2 cups broccoli florets
2 cups fresh snow peas
1 cup chicken or vegetable stock
1 cup coconut milk
1 tablespoon green curry paste
1 teaspoon fresh grated ginger
¼ cup fresh mint chopped

Directions:

1. Set up and prepare the slow cooker.
2. Place the lamb in the slow cooker, followed by the apple, green bell pepper, celery. If possible add the broccoli, and snow peas in the last 30-45 minutes of cooking, otherwise add it at the same time..
3. In a bowl combine the chicken or vegetable stock, coconut milk, green curry paste, ginger, and mint. Mix well and add to the slow cooker.
4. Cover and cook for 4 hours on LOW, or 6 hours on HIGH.

Nutritional information:
Calories 339
Total fat 18 g, saturated fat 12 g
Net carbohydrates 13 g

Protein 28 g

Variety of Vegetables

Who says that low carb living needs to be heavy with meat? Vegetables can be the star of a low carb meal just as easily as any meat. All you need is to know which vegetables to use and how to bring out the best flavors. These unique vegetable dishes will help you do just that.

Mexican Mock Mac and Cheese

Cook Time: 2 hours
Prep Time: 10 minutes
Serves: 4-6

Ingredients:
1 large head cauliflower, cut into small florets
2 cloves garlic, crushed and minced
1 cup tomatoes, diced
1 cup Monterey jack cheese, shredded
1 cup Cotija cheese, crumbled
½ cup cream cheese
1 cup vegetable or chicken stock
1 cup heavy cream
2 teaspoons ancho chili powder
1 teaspoon cumin
¼ cup fresh cilantro, chopped
1 teaspoon salt
1 teaspoon black pepper

Directions:

1. Set up and prepare your slow cooker.
2. Add the cauliflower, garlic, tomatoes, and vegetable stock.
3. Cover and cook for 2 hours on HIGH.

4. In a bowl, combine the Monterey jack cheese, Cotija cheese, cream cheese, heavy cream, ancho chili powder, cumin, cilantro, salt, and black pepper. Mix well.
5. About half an hour before you are ready to eat, stir the cheese mixture into the slow cooker until evenly distributed.
6. Cover and continue cooking until heated through.

Nutritional information:
Calories 459
Total fat 40 g, saturated fat 24 g
Net carbohydrates 9 g
Protein 16 g

Creamy Cabbage Au Gratin

Cook Time: 2 hours
Prep Time: 10 minutes
Serves: 4

Ingredients:
4 cups cabbage, shredded
1 cup carrots, peeled and sliced thinly
½ cup scallions, sliced
½ cup vegetable stock
½ cup milk
1 egg, beaten
½ cup fontina cheese, shredded
½ cup Swiss cheese, shredded
¼ cup fresh parsley, chopped
2 tablespoons fresh chives, chopped
1 teaspoon salt
1 teaspoon black pepper

Directions:

1. Set up and prepare your slow cooker.
2. Mix the cabbage, carrots, scallions, vegetable stock, milk, and egg in the slow cooker.
3. Cover and cook on HIGH for 2 hours.
4. Half an hour before you are ready to eat, add the fontina cheese, Swiss cheese, parsley, chives, salt, and black pepper.
5. Cover and continue cooking until the cheese is melted.

Nutritional information:
Calories 227
Total fat 14 g, saturated fat 8 g,
Net carbohydrates 8 g

Protein 15 g

Rustic Squash Bake

Cook Time: 4 hours
Prep Time: 10 minutes
Serves: 6

Ingredients:
4 cups butternut squash, peeled and cubed
1 cup acorn squash, peeled and cubed
1 cup yellow onion, diced
1 cup bacon, cooked and crumbled (optional)
1 ½ cups vegetable stock
½ cup unsweetened apple juice
½ cup pecans, chopped
1 teaspoon thyme
1 teaspoon nutmeg
1 teaspoon salt
1 teaspoon black pepper

Directions:

1. Set up and prepare your slow cooker.
2. Add the butternut squash to the slow cooker, followed by the acorn squash, yellow onion and bacon.
3. Add in the vegetable stock and apple juice.
4. Next, add the pecans and season with thyme, nutmeg, salt and black pepper.
5. Cover and cook for 4 hours on LOW.

Nutritional information:
Calories 176
Total fat 9 g, saturated fat 1 g
Net carbohydrates 15 g
Protein 4 g

Spaghetti Squash with Mushrooms and Peppers

Cook Time: 4 hours
Prep Time: 10 minutes
Serves: 4-6

Ingredients:
4 cups spaghetti squash (insides only)
2 cloves garlic, crushed and minced
3 cups cremini mushrooms, halved or quartered
1 cup red bell pepper, diced
1 cup walnuts, chopped
2 cups vegetable stock
1 sprig fresh rosemary
1 tablespoon fresh dill, chopped
1 tablespoon fresh chives, chopped
1 teaspoon salt
1 teaspoon black pepper
½ cup goat cheese, crumbled

Directions:
1. Set up and prepare your slow cooker.
2. In the slow cooker, combine the spaghetti squash, garlic, cremini mushrooms, red bell pepper, and walnuts.
3. Next, add the vegetable stock and season with rosemary, dill, chives, salt and black pepper.
4. Cover and cook for 4 hours on LOW.
5. Half an hour before you are ready to eat, remove the lid and add the goat cheese and stir. Cover and continue cooking

Nutritional information:
Calories 334
Total fat 27 g, saturated fat 6 g

Net carbohydrates 13 g
Protein 13 g

Creamy Spinach and Artichoke Casserole

Cook Time: 4 hours
Prep Time: 10 minutes
Serves: 6

Ingredients:
12 cups fresh spinach, torn
2 cups artichoke hearts, quartered
1 cup red onion, diced
3 cloves garlic, crushed and minced
1 ½ cups vegetable stock
1 tablespoon butter, diced
1 teaspoon crushed red pepper flakes
1 tablespoon fresh dill, chopped
¼ cup fresh parsley, chopped
1 teaspoon salt
1 teaspoon white pepper
1 cup walnuts, chopped
1 cup sour cream
1 cup Swiss cheese, shredded
½ cup goat cheese, crumbled
¼ cup fresh grated Parmesan cheese

Directions:

1. Set up and prepare your slow cooker.
2. In the slow cooker, mix the artichoke hearts, red onion, garlic, vegetable stock, and butter.
3. Season with the crushed red pepper flakes, dill, parsley, salt and white pepper.
4. Cover and cook on LOW for 4 hours.
5. Half an hour before you are ready to eat, remove the lid and add the spinach, walnuts, sour cream, Swiss cheese,

goat cheese, and Parmesan. Mix until well blended.
6. Cover and continue cooking until ready to serve.

Nutritional information:
Calories 388
Total fat 32 g, saturated fat 13 g
Net carbohydrates 11 g
Protein 15 g

Slow Cooked Ratatouille

Cook Time: 4 hours
Prep Time: 10 minutes
Serves: 4-6

Ingredients:
2 cups canned tomatoes, with liquid
3 tablespoons tomato paste
1 ½ cups vegetable stock
3 cloves garlic, crushed and minced
4 cups eggplant, peeled and cubed
4 cups zucchini, sliced
2 cups summer squash, peeled and sliced
1 cup green bell pepper, diced
1 cup red onion, diced
2 teaspoons Italian seasoning
1 teaspoon onion powder
1 teaspoon salt
1 teaspoon black pepper

Directions:

1. Set up and prepare your slow cooker.
2. In the slow cooker, combine the canned tomatoes with liquid, tomato paste, and vegetable stock.
3. Add the garlic, eggplant, zucchini, summer squash, green bell pepper, and onion.
4. Season with the Italian seasoning, onion powder, salt, and black pepper.
5. Cover and cook on LOW for 4 hours.

Nutritional information:
Calories 119
Total fat 1 g, saturated fat 0 g

Net carbohydrates 15 g
Protein 5 g

Green Bean and Mushroom Casserole

Cook Time: 4 hours
Prep Time: 10 minutes
Serves: 6

Ingredients:
8 cups fresh green beans, trimmed
2 cups fresh mushrooms, sliced
1 cup water chestnuts, drained and chopped
1 cup yellow onion, diced
2 tablespoons butter, diced
1 ½ cups vegetable stock
1 tablespoon soy sauce
1 teaspoon crushed red pepper flakes
1 tablespoon fresh chives, chopped
1 teaspoon garlic powder
¼ cup fresh parsley, chopped
1 cup sour cream
½ cup heavy cream
½ cup Parmesan cheese
Sliced almonds, for garnish if desired

Directions:

1. Set up and prepare your slow cooker.
2. In the slow cooker combine, the green beans, mushrooms, water chestnuts, yellow onion, and butter. Toss to mix.
3. In a bowl, combine the vegetable stock, soy sauce, crushed red pepper flakes, chives, and garlic powder.
4. Cover and cook on LOW for 4 hours.
5. Half an hour before you are ready to eat, remove the lid and stir in the parsley, sour cream, heavy cream, and

Parmesan. Continue cooking until heated through.
6. Serve garnished with almond sliced.

Nutritional information:
Calories 307
Total fat 22 g, saturated fat 14 g
Net carbohydrates 15 g
Protein 9 g

Printed in Dunstable, United Kingdom